A Nineteenth-Century Garden

As It Is   AN UNPLEASANT HOME
BEFORE PATRONIZING THE NURSERYMEN.

As It Will Be   A PLEASANT HOME
AFTER PATRONIZING THE TREE DEALERS.

"The parable of Jones and Bown," published with the print, explains that the improvements were made possible by profits from an orchard. Colored lithograph, c. 1870, 22.3 × 13.7 cm, D. H. Dewey, *The Nurseryman's Specimen Book of American Horticulture and Floriculture, Fruits, Flowers, Ornamental Trees, Shrubs, Roses, &c.,* c. 1880.

A Nineteenth-Century Garden

CHARLES VAN RAVENSWAAY

A Main Street Press Book

UNIVERSE BOOKS   New York

Published by Universe Books
381 Park Avenue South
New York City 10016

Produced by The Main Street Press
42 Main Street
Clinton, New Jersey 08809

Printed in the United States of America

Cover design by Quentin Fiore

Cover photograph and illustrations, George J. Fistrovich

Acknowledgments

Many helpful friends made this book possible and their aid, so generously given, is acknowledged here with the greatest pleasure. Mrs. Robert Baschnagel, Rochester, New York, provided biographical information on D. M. Dewey and others active in the colored plate field. Additional research data was supplied by Mrs. Bernard E. Harkness, Geneva, New York. Mrs. Elmer Gregory, Rhineland, Missouri, sent notes on her grandfather, Samuel Miller. Elizabeth Woodburn, Hopewell, New Jersey, was, as always, helpful in many ways. Members of the Winterthur Museum Staff, Anne F. Clapp and E. McSherry Fowble, analyzed the colored plates to determine the processes used in making them, and George J. Fistrovich captured their beauty with his sensitive photography. The first draft of the manuscript was reviewed by Dr. George B. Tatum of the University of Delaware faculty, who suggested helpful changes in references to garden design, and by Dr. Henry T. Skinner, Bowie, Maryland, who advised on botanical nomenclature. The final draft was greatly improved by the editing skills of Janet H. Baker, Media, Pennsylvania. To these and others who aided in various ways, I am most appreciative.

Charles van Ravenswaay
May, 1977

"Garden Plan in the *Natural and Graceful Style*," J. J. Thomas, *Illustrated Annual Register of Rural Affairs for 1855* (1856).

Nineteenth Century
American Gardens

The average American had little time or taste for gardening until well into the nineteenth century, for his country was new and other more practical needs demanded attention. Even the growing of vegetables was limited by nineteenth-century standards. Of the great colonial gardens, most were in the South, both in the English colonies and in those of France and Spain along the Gulf, where slaves provided the labor that was so scarce and expensive elsewhere. To the North such gardens as those in Boston of Joseph Barrell with its "marble figures as large as life," and of Thomas Hancock, were as exceptional as some in New York and Philadelphia. Near the latter, Belmont, the country seat of the Peters family, had "parterres and arbours made of yew clipped into forms," and at Woodlands, William Hamilton created a garden before the end of the century which was notable for its collection of rare plant material. In general, however, there was little interest in gardens or gardening, as foreign visitors frequently commented.

Jefferson, among others, had introduced the taste for gardens in which flowers, shrubs, and trees were blended together to provide a parklike setting, but this idea of landscaping the grounds around one's house was not often developed until well into the 1800s. Instead the eighteenth century flower garden (or "pleasure garden" as it was usually called), generally remained a separate domain: fences and plantings to hide the busy, often slovenly activities carried on near the house, whether on a farm or a town lot. The great gardens were often under the care of European gardeners, usually indentured servants. From these great estates the gardens shaded downward in pretensions to dooryard plantings. These smaller gardens were usually designed and tended by the women of the household, as they continued to be in the following century. On farms, or in towns where space permitted, there often orchards and vegetable gardens too.

7

During the nineteenth century, the flower gardens in America, like those elsewhere, went through many permutations brought about by changing fads and fancies. In the middle of the century there was an obsessive interest in cultivating fine fruit and exotic plants. Theories of "taste" in garden design, often vaguely defined, along with increasing affluence and a fluid society, resulted in many lavish gardens which lacked the personal qualities of earlier ones. In time the cycle of taste changed, as it always does, bringing a renewal of interest in "old-fashioned" gardens during the 1890s. Welcoming that change was Charles Sprague Sargent, the first director of the Arnold Arboretum in Boston and a respected author and editor. In an affectionate tribute to the old gardens he had known in his youth fifty years earlier, published in *Garden and Forest*, July 1895, Sargent spoke of them as having been created by toil and love so that the result appealed to the mind as well as the eye. Plants crowded closely upon one another, spilling over the straight walks with masses of color and perfume, and in unexpected corners there was "a wild charm and lonely grace," making them places for dreaming. Although Sargent mentioned many flowers that had been grown fifty years before, it was the quality of these gardens and the mood they created that he remembered best, and he hoped that their subtle qualities would be appreciated by the "dry young Americans" of the 1890s, who, he felt, scorned sentiment and seemed "all for amusement and reform, and precious little for reflection or imagination."

Sargent also chided the new generation of gardeners for their obsession with growing perfect specimens and new varieties, and for smugly thinking that they knew a great deal more about horticulture than their forebears. Actually, he said, citing the old catalogs as evidence, there was probably more variety in the old gardens than in those of the 1890s, and catalogs of the middle 1800s not only listed the great assortment of plant material then available, but also expressed an enthusiasm for gardening shared by the dealers with their customers. Not everyone was caught up in this enthusiasm, however. Dirt farmers and laboring men, many of whom worked twelve or more hours a day and often six days a week, had no time or energy for gardening and no patience with armchair gardeners who proclaimed it to be healthful and morally uplifting.

The first catalogs published in America appeared as broadsides or small pamphlets offering at best a few hundred items, but by 1860 those of the large firms listed several thousand. The change came rapidly, for events of the times stimulated minds and actions, including an interest in horticulture.

This horticultural interest was one of the many side effects of changes in American life and attitudes. The nation had rapidly grown in population and wealth. With increased leisure for many in the older states came an interest in cultural affairs, including town and home beautification. Everywhere there was a new sense of national destiny, of idealism and optimism. The flag had reached the Pacific, and thousands of pioneers were moving west to tame the last frontiers. Their homesteads in the new states and territories required orchards and vegetables, and the amenities of trees and flowers. These settlements had first been accessible only by covered wagon and horseback, but now the railroads and steamboats were destroying that isolation. The nation itself was being drawn closer to Europe by transatlantic steamships which made the Boston to Liverpool run in only fourteen days, making English nursery stock readily available to American growers. In the towns and cities springing up along the routes of settlement and commerce, stores offering seeds and nurseries supplying trees and shrubs began to appear. These western firms soon found themselves in competition with the large eastern houses that sought to exploit the growing national market while serving the increasing number of customers in the East. There many of the rich were building suburban estates and enjoying the pleasures of developing grounds, laying out gardens and orchards, and often building large greenhouses for the tender exotics that had become so fashionable, particularly camellias and Asiatic azaleas. These customers eagerly sought new plants, both the beautiful and the useful, which the suppliers provided from the almost bewildering number of plants being collected throughout the world. Leading American nurserymen and seedsmen regularly visited Europe to keep in touch with new developments; William R. Prince, whose family's nursery at Flushing, Long Island, had been famous since the eighteenth century, even went on a plant-collecting expedition to California between 1849 and 1851.

Among the hundreds of plants introduced were varieties of cannas, clematis, cockscomb, coreopsis, coleus, gladiolus, Japanese lilies, and pampas grass. Annuals, which had not been as frequently grown as perennials, came to have great popularity. In lawns and gardens, the exotic ailanthus, Japanese maple, paulownia, cedar of Lebanon, and Atlas cedar, among many others, grew happily alongside the more familiar native trees which Americans were also beginning to appreciate. A similar increase was seen in the number and variety of vegetables being grown. No longer did a few standard varieties suffice; one catalog of 1865 offered a choice of twenty-four varieties of cabbage, thirteen of beets, and nineteen of lettuce. Rhubarb, generally called "pie-plant," appeared in many gardens.

These introductions gave plant breeders in America and Europe the opportunity to create improved varieties, transforming such flowers as dahlias, petunias, and zinnias from their rather uninteresting native forms into Cinderellas of the plant world. Similarly, many vegetables were improved. One of

9

these was the tomato, which had been grown in Florida and by the French in the Mississippi Valley since the 1700s, and somewhat later in Virginia and neighboring states, despite the widely-held belief that the "Love Apple," as it was called, was poisonous.

This wealth of new plant material became known through various channels, along with the latest scientific data on plant culture, soils, plant diseases, and insect pests, subjects about which the preceding generations had had only empirical knowledge. Each decade saw an increase in the number of farm and garden books by American authors, most of them written by men with much practical knowledge. Gardening magazines appeared, many short-lived, the best of them distinguished for the quality and variety of their contents and for their idealism. Charles Mason Hovey's *Magazine of Horticulture* (1835-1869) reflected a scholarly New England point of view. In *The Horticulturist and Journal of Rural Art and Rural Taste* (1846-1876), the first editor, Andrew Jackson Downing, gave much space to architecture and landscape design. Farmers and their wives found useful articles on fruits and berries, vegetables, and flowers in the new agricultural magazines. Of great public interest were the agricultural and horticultural societies, the first of which had been organized in the 1790s and by 1870 were found throughout the nation. They demonstrated the benefits of better horticultural practices by offering premiums for the best specimens exhibited at their fairs. These exciting annual events, with opportunities to be entertained as well as educated, were the high point each year for many families. Those with specialized interests formed national organizations like the American Pomological Society, dating from 1848.

Of all branches of horticulture, fruit growing was of the greatest interest to most Americans and had been since early in the colonial period. Fruits were a welcome addition to the limited diet of the average family, particularly apples and pears, for they could be dried, made into cider, or kept fresh to be eaten during the winters. Most colonial orchards consisted of seedling trees generally bearing scruffy, sour fruit; better varieties had to be imported from Europe or, by the late 1700s, bought from the few American nurseries then established. Even in 1810 only four or five nurseries of any consequence were said to have existed, and they were by no means profitable. But matters improved. By 1844 the Prince Nursery had 420 varieties of apples for sale. In Virginia the Staunton Nursery offered 343 varieties in 1858, especially those productive in the South. Better types of other fruits, along with berries, became more widely grown near the middle of the century. When improved varieties of grapes were developed that grew well in America, they too entered family gardens and were the basis of a flourishing wine industry.

Near the middle of the century, the lists of ornamentals offered by the leading nurseries reached lengths which seem astonishing today. In the Prince catalog of 1844 were 348 varieties of herbaceous perennial flowering plants, along with 294 camellias, 115 geraniums, 13 herbaceous peonies and 42 tree peonies, 106 carnations, 56 pinks, 112 Chinese chrysanthemums, 58 iris, 14 day lilies, 65 phlox, and 1,253 roses.

In the new states and territories, pioneer nurserymen were at work collecting, testing, and even hybridizing plant material that would meet their often rugged climates. H. A. Congar, who operated the Whitewater Garden & Nursery in Wisconsin, addressed his 1860 catalog to his "Respected Friends" and went on to mention "such hardy items . . . as the returning confidence in the ultimate success in Wisconsin seems to demand." In addition to the usual fruits and berries that would survive in the northern climate, he listed deciduous and evergreen trees, and shrubs, vines, roses, dahlias, peonies, phloxes, and bulbous roots. There were also a few surprises, such as sweet potato plants and "osier, or basket willow," the last in deference to the German settlers of his state who preferred willow baskets to those of splints. In Minnesota, the modest catalog issued in 1872 by Lewis Martin of the Anoka Nursery announced that he aimed "to furnish everything that is found to be hardy and reliable for our climate and soil." He recommended only fifteen varieties of apples that would survive the extreme cold of the region and a small number of plums, cherries, grapes, currants, gooseberries, raspberries, and strawberries. His list of ornamentals was even more modest, being limited to "snow balls," two varieties of lilacs, and "assorted roses." Heat and drought made horticulture difficult in West Texas. There, about 1874, G. Onderdonk bravely started the Mission Valley Nurseries in Victoria County, on the bank of the Guadalupe River. He admitted in his fall catalog three years later that he "started quite in the dark to explore the great field of Western and Southern Texas Horticulture. We had no precedents to guide us. We groped from one point to another" but, he added cheerfully, "The more we explore this branch of Southern horticulture, the richer and more abundant are our rewards." Although Onderdonk was particularly interested in peaches that would do well in his area, he also supplied other fruits, including pomegranates, oranges, and lemons. For flower gardens he had a choice of 37 roses, crape myrtles, "spirea bridle wreath," and "yellow jassamine."

In the early 1800s firms dealing in plant material often combined selling seeds and bulbs with greenhouse plants and nursery stock, the last representing the bulk of their sales. The small amount of flower seeds then sold is suggested by the 1824 catalog of David and Cuthbert Landreth, a Philadelphia firm established in 1792, which mentioned having an extensive and handsome assortment of flower seeds but thought them of too little interest to list. Instead they devoted many pages to vegetable seed, with an eye, apparently, to the Pennsylvania-German farmers, who were famous for their produce. One of the many now-forgotten vegetables they included was "Scurvey Grass," whose only virtue must have been its reputed medicinal value, for the leaves, eaten as a salad, were acrid and bitter. The catalog included the English and botanical names of each item, as other firms had begun doing, but also added their "place of nativity," suggesting how early the firms sought to make their catalogs interesting and informative. Later they went to surprising lengths, combining catalogs with almanacs, making them into quasi-magazines, and most of all being chatty and personal so that in time the heads of those firms came to seem like personal friends in many households. "I order my seeds from Mr. Vick" or "Mr. Henderson says" became commonplace expressions.

By the 1840s many firms specializing in seeds and bulbs had appeared. B. K. Bliss of Springfield, Massachusetts (and later New York City), described 676 varieties of flower seeds in 1858, and 1,612 seven years later—everything from *Abronia* (sand verbena) to *Vinca* (periwinkle)—and an assortment of vegetables probably larger than those found in any catalog today, including many that are no longer grown. Nasturtiums were listed in both the flower and the vegetable sections because the seedpods were then pickled for use as capers and the stems, leaves, and blossoms used in salads.

Although some firms began to grow part of their seed, a practice that gradually expanded, most of them relied on European growers. James Vick of Rochester, New York, who combined a love of flowers with a phenomenal zeal in promoting their sale, boasted that his seeds came from the best growers in France, Germany, and England and that "every *Novelty* that appears in any part of the world is obtained immediately." He, like many of his competitors, provided much information on plant culture, offered discounts for group purchases, and sent orders postpaid. By 1872 he claimed that his catalog was being mailed to 225,000 people. Vick and others also sold farm and garden equipment, weather vanes, fertilizers, and spray material.

The interest in new plants and seeds was insatiable. In 1872 Peter Henderson & Company, of New York City reflected this by publishing a separate catalog, *New Plants for 1872*; many of the regular catalogs had at least a section listing the novelties for each year.

The midwestern seed houses also had a rapid growth. In Detroit the D. M. Ferry & Company's catalog grew to more than 200 pages within less than twenty years after its founding in 1856. "The increase of gardening in all its branches on this continent is marvelous," the editor exulted in 1875, "and yet our people have made but a beginning!" He went on to laud the growing of flowers as a reflection of the culture and refinement of the age, and of raising vegetables as a profitable activity. Then followed sixty pages devoted to listing vegetable seeds and a hundred pages to flowers, all profusely illustrated.

West Coast plant needs and interests were stressed in the assortment of seeds, trees, plants, and bulbs sold by E. E. Moore in San Francisco in 1871, which included all those of "known excellence, as adapted to the various localities of this country, and adjacent States." Most of the familiar varieties were represented, along with forty-two varieties of sweet, pot, and medicinal herb seeds. He also sold opium poppy seed (to be grown for medicinal purposes) and seeds of native California plants.

The garden plans of middle-class Americans during the first decades of the nineteenth century followed those of earlier years. The locations of flower and

"An Old-Fashioned, or *Geometric Style* of Garden. From an Old Print," A. J. Downing, *Treatise on the Theory and Practice of Landscape Gardening* (1859).

13

"The Beautiful in Landscape Gardening," A. J. Downing, *Treatise on the Theory and Practice of Landscape Gardening* (1859).

vegetable gardens and orchards were selected for their convenience and appropriateness in relation to the house and other structures. Soil, drainage, exposure, and the space available were also primary considerations. All these elements influenced the actual design, so that generally form followed function instead of being arbitrarily imposed. The plan was completed by enclosing the gardens with wooden fences or, less often, with brick walls or hedges, to keep out wandering animals and provide support for vines and climbing roses. Fruit trees, often in dwarf form, were scattered in the flower beds or espaliered against the walls. The effect of these individual creations was that of an orderly plan combined with a happy and somewhat undisciplined profusion of plants. So common was this type of garden until after the mid-1800s, and so frequently were the beds edged with boxwood, that one suspects many so-called colonial gardens actually date from after that period.

Around 1840 garden and landscape designs in the "natural and graceful style" came into fashion, which, among other concepts, emphasized the use of exotic plant material and the place of the individual plant and tree in the total design. Calling such landscaping "the modern, or gardenesque style" at first, writers hastened to explain that gardens were not intended to be "a rude imitation of nature, without any appearance of art," but that they should represent "the cognizance of art in every part," an explanation that must have bewildered

14

many readers. It remained for Andrew Jackson Downing (1815-1852) to clarify those theories. His *Treatise on the Theory and Practice of Landscape Gardening, Adapted to North America*, first published in 1841, went through many editions. The following year his *Cottage Residences* appeared. Both served a large audience that wished, as Downing said, to ornament their grounds and embellish their places, but needed some "leading principles" with which they would find it comparatively easy to produce delightful and satisfactory results. These he offered in such a charming manner and with such success that he became the taste-maker of the period, not only in landscape design but also in architecture and furnishings.

Downing felt that in landscape design there were three general styles. The old-fashioned or "geometric" style, in which regularity and symmetry were the distinguishing features, was still appropriate for public gardens or squares and for old houses. The two new styles took their themes from nature itself. These were—to paraphrase his elaborate definitions—the "Beautiful," in which nature was shown under considerable control, and the "Picturesque," which artfully created the irregular, rude, and more violent aspects of nature. Recommended

"The Picturesque in Landscape Gardening," A. J. Downing, *Treatise on the Theory and Practice of Landscape Gardening* (1859).

"The Excelsior Lawn Mower," one of four models of handmowers and several horse-powered mowers, made by Chadborn & Caldwell, Newburgh, New York, in 1877. *American Agriculturist* (1877).

plans for the latter show flowers in irregularly shaped beds along winding walks and massed in borders against background plantings, rather than relegated to a separate flower garden. Whatever style was chosen, Downing warned that its success depended upon the exercise of "taste."

The new suburban estates soon embodied in their buildings and grounds the romantic theories of Downing and his fellow landscape designers. Trees and shrubs were carefully grouped for effect, and vistas created or enhanced. For the first time there were lawns as we know them today, made possible by the mowers that came into use during the 1850s. These mechanical aids banished from grounds and gardens the unsightly stubble of weeds and coarse wild grasses that had been only partially kept under control with scythes, a laborious task requiring much skill to close-crop. With the use of the lawn mower, bluegrass and other lawn grasses could be grown and mowed to a velvety texture, creating a revolution in home beautification. It also brought pleasant changes in social customs. People were now enticed out of doors and from their verandas more frequently during the warmer months to enjoy the grass and flowers, play croquet, and to rest on cast-iron seats or "rustic" wooden benches and in airy summerhouses. Cast-iron fountains, figures, and even birdhouses added to the furnishings of these out-of-door living rooms. Flower beds were made dramatic by large exotic plants such as palms, banana trees, and cannas, with their vivid blossoms. Edged with wire or brick, beds of annuals, particularly verbenas, which were then very popular, were like bright bouquets set in the greensward.

Such extravagances enjoyed by the affluent and the fashion-conscious influenced others, who borrowed elements from the romantic style when it suited their purposes and their tastes. Some, however, ignored it. In Louisiana many of the Creole gardens were laid out in the French style; other gardens, like those of the princely Valcour Aime in St. James Parish, were laid out in the English style. In the Aime garden (which had an English head gardener) was a great collection of plants, trees, and shrubs, along with hothouses and ornamental buildings. Among the surprises to be seen at *"le petit Versailles,"* as it was often called, was a miniature river, and a pagoda set on a mound covered with violets. But in all of these gardens the profligacy of nature in that subtropical climate produced results quite different from those originally intended. Similarly the Charles L. Bell garden on Lake Ponchartrain seemed like a vast conservatory to a visitor in 1858. There the dark foliage of treelike flowering shrubs provided a background for colorful plants, all contributing to the heavy fragrance. At Natchez, Mississippi, also in 1858, the garden of Dr. Mercer at Laurel Hill was filled with camellias and blossoming trees. Roses grew so profusely that a white Lady Banks rose had a stem twenty-one inches in circumference, and red roses festooned pine trees to heights of forty feet. The Andrew Brown garden covered seven acres. There were walks among the plantings, "thousands of roses," evergreen arbors and screens: and in the garden proper, with its long vista, each bed was bordered with dwarf pompon roses a few inches in height which bloomed throughout most of the year.

"Gothic Settee," made by Hutchinson & Wickersham, New York City, c. 1858. J. J. Thomas, *Illustrated Annual Register of Rural Affairs* (1869).

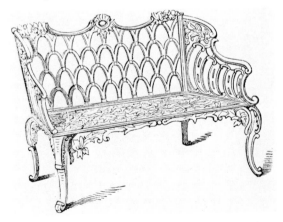

17

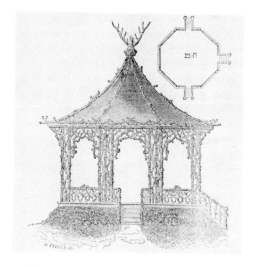

"Cast-Iron *Rustic* Summer House,"
made by the Robert Wood Foundry,
Philadelphia, 1856. *Horticulturist*
(June, 1856).

Spectacular as these great gardens were, it was the modest efforts of countless anonymous gardeners that showed how widespread the interest in gardening had become. The results could be seen everywhere. A farmhouse near Concord, New Hampshire, had "a little border of double pinks, balsams, asters, petunias, and many other pretty flowers." Dr. S. P. Hildreth described dooryards in the older Ohio settlements decorated with "rose-bushes, snow-balls and altheas; while the fronts and door-ways are covered with the wide-spread branches of the wild *Rosa rubra*, or *multiflora* of the West. The *Bignonia radicans*, native trumpet-flower, or the tri-colored honeysuckle . . . is sometimes seen mounting the roofs of our cabins."

After the Civil War, horticulture continued to reflect changes in American life, of which it had become an accepted part. Landscape design had matured because of the work of such skilled practitioners as Frederick Law Olmsted (1822-1903), the principal designer of Central Park in New York who also created many other parks throughout the country and designed many private estates. American towns and villages had matured, too. The years of growth and bustle were a memory; time had brought tree-shaded streets and small home gardens bright with flowers. In the South the once great gardens had disappeared from neglect as a casualty of the war; elsewhere others were destroyed by the growth of cities and the spread of industry. Something of the creativity and excitement that had once made gardening so interesting seemed to be fading, along with the passing of the colorful personalities who had once dominated the seed and nursery trade.

Then in the 1890s came a change, as we have seen. Gardens reminiscent of an earlier America appeared, along with colonial-style buildings painted in fresh, bright colors. Antique collecting increased. In the South many of the abandoned, almost forgotten old gardens were re-created. Not only America, but the Old World, provided garden designs suggesting traditional elegance—and sentiment, as Sargent wished—with those in Florida and southern California being inspired by the Spanish-colonial heritage. As a prophet of more wonders to come in the horticultural world, the plant wizard Luther Burbank was busy with his magic in California, creating new vegetables, fruits, and flowers, and gardeners looked forward to the new century with high hopes.

"Entrance to the H. P. McKean Estate, North Philadelphia Plank Road, Pennsylvania, 1859." The wooden gates, painted a dark green, were set in a stone wall. *Gardener's Monthly* (Jan., 1859).

Fruit and Flower Plates

The plates of fruits, trees, shrubs, and flowers shown on the following pages are a sampling from the many published in Rochester, New York, from the late 1850s until sometime in the early 1870s. They were not intended as botanical studies or for home decoration but were bound into books to aid "tree peddlers"—as the agents of nurseries were disparagingly called—in selling plants to farmers and villagers. The earliest of these plates were fairly large (12 by 9 inches untrimmed). These proved unwieldy, so plates were made for smaller pocket-sized books of about 9½ by 5¾ inches. The name of the peddler and the nursery he represented, were stamped on the leather binding to add an official tone to his activities.

Considering the poor reputation these men then enjoyed throughout rural America because of their sharp practices, they needed whatever prestige could be mustered, along with a glib tongue and considerable physical endurance. These plates proved a bonanza. One can imagine a peddler visiting isolated farm homes, casually flipping through his book to tantalize housewives with glimpses of wonderful flowers or capturing the interest of suspicious, taciturn farmers with visions of orchards bending under a load of luscious fruit. That these plates idealized the products of nature does not seem to have been questioned by the unwary or to have troubled the publishers. Some of the fruits were shown as little more than abstractions, with the colors shading from the faintest blush to the most vivid reds. The foliage was always richly green and miraculously free from pests. In addition, the earliest and most completely detailed plates had subtle highlights and a sheen on the fruits, creating an effect so mouth-watering that they seemed to be fresh from the fabled gardens of the Hesperides.

Although created for commercial use, these plates were also an innovation in American popular art. Forgotten today and little collected, their artistic qualities command respect. The techniques used in producing them were essentially traditional, which may have been one of the reasons for their original success. To the average American of the time, scarcely aware of fashionable art, these plates, with their simplified designs and sparkling colors, were akin to the stylized art with which he was familiar: the stenciled chairs, the portraits by itinerant, unschooled artists, and the flower and fruit paintings by schoolgirls.

Different techniques were used in making these plates, perhaps in an effort to find better ways of mass-producing them. Some of the earliest appear to have been almost completely freehand watercolors. Others were theorem paintings made with stencils through which color was applied in several different ways, with the details added freehand. (For many years ladies had used this method to create pictures of fruits and flowers.) Still other plates had the outlines faintly lithographed or engraved so that the colors could be more easily laid on freehand. A lesser number—and these were certainly the least expensive and the least dramatic—were lithographs printed in one or two colors. On all plates the subject was identified, most with the imprint of the publisher. At a slight extra cost a nursery could have its name added. Some of the first plates have handwritten titles, a practice necessary because the same plate was used to illustrate two or three different subjects which were similar enough to pass muster with different coloring or a slight rearrangement of some of the parts. This kind of trickery was possible because many of the plants being sold were so new that the public could not recognize the subterfuge.

One would like to know more about the artists who created the original designs, but few of their names have survived. At least some of their designs were copied for pin money by the many art-minded ladies then living in Rochester, whose skills varied considerably and who were not above adding their individual touches. We wish, too, that we knew the sources used by the artists in their work. Some were drawn from nature, but many of the plates appear to have been copied, or adapted, from published sources. Others resemble the flowers ladies had been painting for pleasure, often in the autograph albums of their friends. A few are so oriental in quality (such as the Chinese peonies on p. 41) that the artist may have seen a Chinese or Japanese flower painting.

The success of these plates did not escape the notice of the promotion-minded heads of leading seed and nursery firms. Their industry had pioneered in the mail-order business with descriptive catalogs and by inventing the mail-order blank. In the late 1840s black-and-white illustrations had been added to seed catalogs: colored illustrations were an obvious next step but action was delayed, probably because of the cost. The first to move may have been James Vick, that Rochester seedsman and innovator; his 1864 catalog appeared with a colored lithograph of double zinnias which had only been developed four years earlier. Others soon followed suit. While these illustrations were not as splendid as those made for the peddlers, they were well designed and colorful and stimulated sales.

The man credited with having originated the peddlers' plates, and who pioneered in their production and sale, was Dellon Marcus Dewey (1819-1889), a native of Cooperstown, New York. Coming to Rochester in about 1838, he became a bookseller and publisher widely known for his interest in horticulture and art. He encouraged local talent, held art shows, and gave lectures. In time he added an art gallery to his bookshop, where he offered books on the fine arts, engravings, lithographs, Fictile ivory, and Parian marble ornaments, along with paintings. He was also interested in architecture, designing a chancel for Christ Church, where he was a communicant for many years.

In 1858, Rochester having become a major center of the nursery business, this energetic man "originated and adapted the Colored fruit plate to the practical use of Nurserymen, in selling their stock," as he stated twenty years later, and sought to make them both beautiful and profitable. In the beginning he seems to have done just that. A sample book with a price list, perhaps his first, appeared in 1859. In it he said that his "fine colored plates are done by the best artists in the United States," and that all of his plates have his name printed on them. He listed some 275 plates of fruits, berries, grapes, nuts, evergreen and ornamental trees, and flowers, including roses. These plates were priced at twenty-five cents each (if the whole collection was bought) and from thirty-seven to seventy-five cents each in lots of one to twenty. In addition, Dewey said that he would soon offer fifty varieties of fruit, cast in wax and colored after nature, at fifty cents each. In 1878 Dewey had over 2,300 titles in his stock of plates which he offered in three sizes: *Large* (9 by 11 inches), the *Pocket Series* (6 by 9 inches), and the *Medium Series* (7 by 10 inches). The buyer could order a special collection made up to suit his needs, or such stock combinations as *The Local Agents' Plate Book*, a pocket-sized book of some forty-two plates, and *The Florists' Specimen Book* with forty-eight, 9 by 11 plates, priced at ten dollars. The prices varied greatly but Dewey asserted he had determined to keep up the quality.

By 1870 Dewey's success had encouraged a number of competitors to enter the fruit plate field. In Rochester they included W. H. Metcalf & Company, John W. Thompson, and D. W. Sargent. Sargent, who had worked as a clerk for Dewey in the 1860s, advertised "Fruit and Flower Plates, 1,000 varieties manufactured and sold" in 1871. Thompson's specialty in 1872 was "hand colored plates." He continued in business until sometime in the 1880s, but by then the artwork that had made such products so popular earlier had given way to cheaper and less dramatic ways of illustrating plant material, including the use of colored wood engravings, many of them produced by George Frauenberger in Rochester.

Chromolithographed plates, produced by Dewey and his competitors, began appearing with increasing frequency during the 1870s. In addition to being less expensive than those hand colored, they were also artistically more in the spirit of the times with softer colors and greater detail. Many of them were produced by the Stecher Lithographic Company of Rochester whose quality work is shown in the plates for *The Horticultural Art Journal* which it published from 1886 to 1891.

When Dewey died in 1889 a writer commented that his name was "almost as familiar as a household word." His business was taken over by M. Brunswick & Company, headed by Minnie Brunswick, formerly an employee of Dewey. She announced in 1890 that all of Dewey's artists had been retained by her firm. By that time, however, the era of the tree peddlers was ending, for they were losing out to the mail-order catalogs and a changing market. Today the peddlers' hand-colored plates remain to remind us of an interesting period in our horticultural history and to delight us for reasons that would have pleased the art-minded Mr. Dewey.

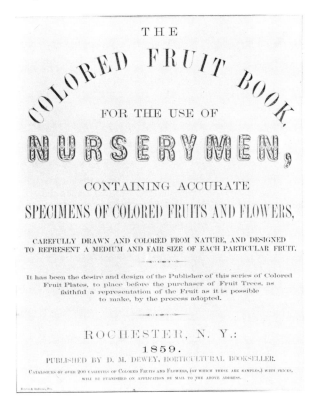

THE

COLORED FRUIT BOOK,

FOR THE USE OF

NURSERYMEN,

CONTAINING ACCURATE

SPECIMENS OF COLORED FRUITS AND FLOWERS,

CAREFULLY DRAWN AND COLORED FROM NATURE, AND DESIGNED TO REPRESENT A MEDIUM AND FAIR SIZE OF EACH PARTICULAR FRUIT.

It has been the desire and design of the Publisher of this series of Colored Fruit Plates, to place before the purchaser of Fruit Trees, as faithful a representation of the Fruit as it is possible to make, by the process adopted.

ROCHESTER, N. Y.:
1859.
PUBLISHED BY D. M. DEWEY, HORTICULTURAL BOOKSELLER.

CATALOGUES OF OVER 200 VARIETIES OF COLORED FRUITS AND FLOWERS, (OF WHICH THESE ARE SAMPLES,) WITH PRICES, WILL BE FURNISHED ON APPLICATION BY MAIL TO THE ABOVE ADDRESS.

When this winter apple was first brought to public notice in the early 1840s, it was soon recognized as one of the finest apples originating in America. It was discovered on the Oliver C. Chapin farm, near East Bloomfield, New York, having grown from a seed brought from Connecticut about 1800. The fine appearance and flavor of its fruit, sold in Rochester about 1841, attracted the attention of Rochester nurserymen Ellwanger and Barry, who sent specimens to the Massachusetts Horticultural Society in May, 1844, where they created something of a sensation. Trees were sought after by nurserymen and orchardists, and within a few years the Northern Spy was being grown in many parts of New England, New York State, and elsewhere, including the Midwest. How and where it received its curious name has been forgotten.

"It is one of the most beautiful apples," Charles Mason Hovey wrote in 1851, "having a rich, deep crimson skin, with purplish stripes, and covered with soft bloom." He and others commented that it ripened in January (apparently a nurseryman's term for when the apples ripened in storage) and "keeps perfectly sound, and retains all its freshness still June," making it valuable for home use as well as export. The flavor is unforgettable, as I remember so vividly from my own boyhood, when I had the freedom of a neighbor's tree. "Delicious, fragrant, and sprightly," Andrew Jackson Downing described it. Another writer, more soberly, reported the "flavor rich, aromatic, mild, sub-acid, fine." Although the fruit is seldom found in the market today, trees are still available for the home orchard.

Northern Spy Apple

Lithograph outline with applied color, c. 1859,
28.7 × 22 cm.

To Robert Fortune, the Scottish plant collector whose Asiatic plant introductions are mentioned so frequently in these pages, gardeners are also indebted for the introduction of two species of the shrub Weigela. The first was a pale pink variety (then named *W. rosea* and now known as *W. florida*) which he found with other plants in a mandarin's garden on the island of Chu Shan, off the China coast, and brought to England in 1846; the second, *W. floribunda*, pictured here, a dark crimson from Japan which he introduced about 1860.

In Fortune's interesting account of finding *W. florida* in the mandarin's garden, called the Grotto because of the rockwork so admired by the Chinese, he spoke of his delight at seeing the "fine rose-colored flowers, which hung in graceful bunches . . . from the branches" and added that the plant should be grown as it was in China, with its natural form retained. In 1851 C. M. Hovey received a plant for his Boston garden and the following year reported that it had stood the winter without injury. He pronounced it "one of the richest acquisitions to our early flowering, hardy, ornamental shrubs." Other growers, in Rochester, New York, and elsewhere, also issued favorable reports.

During the 1860s plant breeders in Belgium developed new varieties of the shrub. All of these were soon offered for sale by American nurseries, but, as the editor of *The American Agriculturist* commented in 1876, "so slow are our people in learning what is good and desirable among trees and shrubs, that plants that have been in cultivation as long as the Weigelas, are still new to the great mass of people." It is true that the shrub was not as widely grown as many others in some parts of America during the nineteenth century, but there may have been reasons other than ignorance of its beauties. The shrub does not take kindly to hot, dry summers like those in the Midwest, but flowers best in cooler and moister parts of the country.

Weigela Florabunda

Weigela floribunda

Theorem painting, watercolor, c. 1870s, 22 ×
14 cm.

*"Weeping Willow. Forsaken. Ask not one to join in
mirth whose heart is desolate."*—The language of
flowers, quoted by Mrs. Almira H. Lincoln in
Familiar Lectures on Botany (1831).

Andrew Jackson Downing, the American horticulturist and landscape designer, visited the Rivers nursery in England in 1850, where he was shown a new variety of a dwarf weeping willow which had been named the "American Weeping Willow." Downing was puzzled by the name, for the tree had come from France; as matters later proved, it was a clone of *Salix purpurea*, which is not native to North America but rather to Europe, North Africa, Central Asia, and Japan. Downing thought that the slender branches falling from a delicate and beautiful round head resembled spray in a fountain and suggested that it be renamed the "Fountain Willow," but Rivers's name stuck. When the tree was introduced into America it seems to have received only modest attention. In some catalogs it was listed as the "North American Weeping Willow."

Willow trees, particularly the weeping varieties, had strong appeal to Victorian taste, which Downing interpreted with sensitivity. He wrote that the Weeping Willow should not be combined with trees expressive of dignity or majesty, such as the oak, where the contrasting forms would create discord in the landscape. Instead, it should be planted on the banks of streams or ponds so that its elegant and graceful form reflected in the water. Most of all, the tree should be grown in cemeteries because of the melancholy, poetical, and scriptural associations connected with it. He felt that the willow expressed grief for the loss of the departed, rather than the darkness of the grave. Continuing in this vein, he described the "light and elegant foliage" flowing "like the dishevelled hair and graceful drapery of a sculptured mourner over a sepulchral urn." The tree, he wrote, "conveys those soothing, though softly melancholy reflections which have made one of our poets exclaim, 'There is a pleasure even in grief.' " Indeed, the most popular motif on tombstones of the period was the carving of a weeping willow sheltering a mourner at a grave.

To create the New American Willow, the species had to be grafted on stock six or seven feet tall. The branches then grew into a pendulous dwarf form. In appearance it was not unlike the Kilmarnock Weeping Willow (*Salix caprea Pendula*) developed in England and introduced to America at about the same time.

The New American Weeping Willow

Salix purpurea Pendula

Lithograph, possibly by T. Sage and Sons,
Buffalo, New York, c. 1859, 28.7 × 22 cm.

It is impossible to imagine an old-fashioned garden without its springtime show of Bleeding Hearts, their graceful racemes of pink blossoms nodding over deep-cut, pale green foliage. It is a hardy herbaceous plant, undemanding in its needs, and gracing borders year after year with its familiar beauty. Luckily the plant breeders have meddled very little with it, so that the flower remains as when Robert Fortune brought it to England in 1846, having found it growing on the island of Chu Shan. He reported that the Chinese called it *Hong-Pah-Moutan-Wha*, which he translated as the "Red and White Moutan Flower," the "Moutan" referring to the similarity of its leaves to those of the Moutan peony, the "king of flowers." By contrast, the common Western name of "Bleeding Heart" seems a rather modest appellation; but it is descriptive and, like the flower itself, caught the public fancy.

The Bleeding Heart first flowered in America in 1851. It is easily propagated and soon became available commercially at the low price of twenty-five cents. Very quickly it became popular throughout the country. Peter Henderson, a nurseryman often given to superlatives, wrote in 1881 that "taking it all in all, it is probably the finest hardy plant in cultivation." By the close of the century it had come to occupy such an established place in American gardens that Liberty Hyde Bailey, the horticulturist and editor, wrote that it provided "one of the choicest memories of old-fashioned gardens" for countless Americans. And so it has remained.

Bleeding Heart

Dicentra spectabilis

Theorem painting, watercolor, c. 1859, 28.7 ×
22 cm.

Robert Fortune, the Scottish traveler and botanist, returned to England in May, 1846, from a three-year plant-collecting trip to China. His sixty-nine plant cases included a shrub which, along with varieties introduced later, was to brighten the last drab days of winter on countless American lawns. At first the shrub was sold by nurserymen as the Japan Golden Bell, or Trinket Flower, but somehow its botanical name became its popular name and Forsythia it remains, memorializing William Forsyth (1737-1804), a director of the Royal Garden at Kensington, England. American horticulturists learned of the shrub in 1846 from British journals. Soon it was being grown in New England and New York and was hailed, both here and abroad, as a remarkable plant, "destined to be one of the greatest ornaments of our garden." And so it became, despite the efforts of some gardeners to restrain this sun- and freedom-loving shrub in crowded, shaded borders or to torture it into clipped hedges.

Fortune wrote that he found the Forsythia in the "grotto garden" of a mandarin living on the island of Chu Shan and that it was a great favorite with the Chinese, being grown in all the gardens of the rich in North China. Later he found specimens growing in the wild in the province of Chekian, "where I thought it even more ornamental in its natural state . . . than when cultivated." Another variety, *Forsythia suspensa*, the "Forsythia, Drooping Yellow" of the first American nurserymen who offered plants, was introduced about 1859 and was reported as an import from Japan of slender and graceful habit, with very long pendant shoots.

Early gardeners also welcomed the bright and fragrant blooms of the ornamental flowering currants, some of which were native to North America. Their blossoms and leaves appeared early in the spring, and their low habit of growth and fresh-green foliage throughout the growing season made them welcome additions to border plantings. But these modest shrubs serve as the alternate hosts for the destructive white-pine blister rust, and many states now have laws prohibiting their growth.

The Ribes Beatone, now *Ribes x gordonianum* (Ribes beatonii), a flowering currant with reddish-yellow blossoms, was originated by a Mr. Beaton, apparently of the Clapton Nursery in England, and was described in British and American publications in 1842. One of its parents was the crimson-flowered currant (*Ribes sanguineum*), a native of the Pacific Northwest which was introduced to British gardens by David Douglas, the plant collector, during the 1820s. The hardy shrub was described as having an erect and graceful habit of growth and producing its fragrant blooms in profusion.

Forsythia and Ribes Beatone

Forsythia viridissima; Ribes x gordonianum (R. beatonii)

Penciled outline, theorem painting (stems), watercolor, c. 1859, 28.7 × 22 cm.

Flowering Almonds, both the tree and dwarf shrub types, have brought their spring bloom to American gardens since the middle of the eighteenth century and perhaps earlier. Of all the plants called by this name, the one most widely grown throughout America has been the dwarf shrub, *Prunus tenella* (?), a native of Russia and introduced into English gardens in 1683. Its double blossoms resemble small roses and are silvery pink when they first open, then deepen to rose. The plant is hardy even under the most adverse conditions. Because it spreads freely by runners, it was possible for gardeners to beg "a start" from their more fortunate neighbors, and it was probably in this way, rather than from nurseries, that the plant was frequently obtained. During the 1840s, Henry Ward Beecher, the minister of powerful voice and commanding presence, published a gardening magazine in Indianapolis. In it he mentioned "this favorite shrub . . . found in all gardens and yards," which, as a later writer said, was hallowed with sentiment and mystery from the fairy tales children wove about it. Beecher also added the useful suggestion that the shrub appears best when planted against a background of evergreens, but few home gardeners had that opportunity.

Beginning about 1835 other flowering almonds with double pink and white blossoms were brought to Europe from Chinese and Japanese gardens, and these were soon available to American growers. The double white-flowering almond shown here was probably a tree rather than a shrub. Beautiful as this species is, it never became as popular as the dwarf double pink shrub introduced earlier, or the pink-flowering tree almond (*Prunus amygdalus communis*).

In the late eighteenth century, the Bartram nursery, near Philadelphia, offered a double-flowered peach which appears to have been the same plant listed by the Linnaean Hill Nursery, Washington, in 1811, but a larger selection was not available until much later. By 1844 Prince's listed six varieties, perhaps the largest number in any American nursery at that time. Eight years later English journals reported that two new double-flowering peaches had been received from China, a double crimson and a double white, but the plants were so rare that they sold for three guineas each. By 1860 American nurseries were offering them for sale at seventy-five cents, along with other varieties. They were among the new introductions of double-flowering peach trees collected by Fortune and others with rose, crimson, white, and camellia-flowered blossoms. The availability of these "magnificent ornamental shrubs" added "an entirely new feature to the garden in early spring."

After the Civil War the flowering peaches received greater attention, and by the 1870s they were frequently recommended in American garden and farm publications. Not only did nurseries along the East Coast aid in furthering their cultivation, but the large collection assembled at the Fruitland Nursery of P. J. Berckmans, at Augusta, Georgia, attracted attention from horticulturists. Unfortunately the flowering peach, like other members of its family, is not long-lived, but its blossoms do provide a dramatic spectacle.

Double White-Flowering Almond
Double Crimson-Flowering Peach

Prunus dulcis (P. amygdalus) Albo=plena:
Prunus persica Rubro-plena

Penciled outline, watercolor, c. 1859, 28.7 ×
22 cm.

Victorian ladies professed a likeness for delicate, modest, and fragrant plants, but the grounds landscaped in the new romantic style surrounding the boldly designed new Italian or Gothic-styled country villas included flower beds intended as eye-catching ornaments amid the greensward. These required brightly colored flowers, qualities which the "dashing and showy" tulips most admirably possessed. Indeed, "nothing in the floral world can equal the dazzling brilliancy and gorgeousness of a bed of good tulips," James Vick wrote with fervor in 1869. Such a display could not fail to mark both the taste and wealth of the owner, for a proper bed was understood to mean one large in size and with the flowers in uniform rows and of uniform height. If one of the plants failed, the gardener was expected to replace it. Beds of 100 by 4 feet were considered ideal. Few could achieve anything that dramatic, but Samuel Walker did in the Boston Public Garden each year from 1836 until 1841, and the displays grown by J. S. Cabot in Salem, Massachusetts, also won much acclaim. Their efforts, and those of others, brought the tulip back into fashion in America after a period of neglect. By the 1870s tulips were being grown everywhere, which encouraged Dutch growers to publish American catalogs and to appoint American agents.

The clear, single-colored varieties preferred today, then considered rather commonplace by the knowing, were selling in 1857 for about two cents each. Those most fashionable were the tall late-blooming varieties with large blossoms of rich, variegated coloring which, as was learned much later, resulted from a virus. These were classified as "Bizarres," which had a yellow ground and were marked with other colors: "Byblooms" (or "Bibloems"), with a white ground and markings in shades of purple; and "Roses," in which shades of red were on a white ground. They sold from sixteen dollars to twenty-five dollars a hundred. Double and parrot tulips, which had been developed by French and Dutch growers in the seventeenth century, were also available.

Tulips are native to Asia Minor, China, Siberia, and Japan and had been cultivated for centuries by the Turks before being brought to Western Europe in the late 1500s. During the 1630s the Dutch became so enamored of the flowers that a tulip mania resulted which finally required government action to quell. Tulips were grown in American gardens during the eighteenth century. In 1806 the Philadelphia nurseryman Bernard M'Mahon stated in his *Gardener's Calendar* that the "glorious flower . . . is now in more general estimation, than any other flower whatever," but that interest faded, to be revived later by Victorian gardeners.

Tulips

Lithograph outline, watercolor, c. 1864, 28.2 ×
22.2 cm.

Until the early nineteenth century, American gardeners had little interest in cultivating the native plants, trees, and shrubs of their continent except those of economic value. Instead, they sought the plants of Western Europe, either because they remembered them with nostalgia or felt they would be useful, or simply because they were fashionable. British horticulturists and botanists, however, eagerly collected the "curious" plants of the New World, aided by a few American botanists and plant collectors whose work they encouraged.

Alexander Garden of Charleston sent seeds of the Fringe tree to London in 1757, and John Bartram, the Pennsylvania Quaker botanist, supplied it over a period of years to other British collectors. It may have been grown in a few American gardens during the eighteenth century, but not until Bernard M'Mahon, the Irish-born Philadelphia nurseryman, recommended it for garden use in 1806 did this "very ornamental shrub" receive public recognition here. Its general acceptance came slowly.

The Fringe tree is native over a wide area: New Jersey and eastern Pennsylvania to West Virginia, southern Ohio, Kentucky, and southern Missouri, and east to central Florida. It rarely grows to more than twenty-five feet with a trunk diameter of eight to ten inches. Often it develops a shrubby growth, with several spreading trunks from a common base, but when growing in isolation it develops a low, rounded top. The bark of its root was thought useful for treating intermittent fevers and other chronic diseases. In South Carolina a decoction of the bark was reported used "in the case of native-born Africans who suffered from yaws or ulcers and sores, which are often rapidly fatal. The decoction given internally and used as a wash gave relief, when everything else failed." But it was the blossoms which were its chief attraction to horticulturists. Thomas Nuttall, the English botanist who spent most of his life studying the flora of America, wrote that when in flower in early summer, "few objects can be seen more singular and elegant; the panicles of pendent flowers with which it is then clad give it the appearance of a mass of snow-white fringe, and, when the flowers fall, the ground seems covered with a carpet of white shreds."

It was named "Fringe tree" at a very early date, but it was also known in different places as the Snow-drop tree, White ash, Old man's beard, Poison ash, Grandfather graybeard, Sunflower tree, Snowflower tree, Flowering ash, and perhaps others, suggesting how the trees' blossoms stirred the imagination of early Americans.

White Fringe Tree

Chionanthus virginicus

White fringe Tree

Theorem painting, watercolor over ink drawing,
c. 1864, 28.2 × 22.2 cm.

The botanical name for this flower, from which the more familiar "peony" comes, memorialized Paeon, the physician of the gods, who, according to legend, was transformed by Pluto into the plant following his death. Throughout antiquity the flower was celebrated for protecting people from enchantment and for driving away evil spirits. In early America the faint memory of its former useful properties may have caused it to be used for treating epilepsy and fits in children.

The first peony species brought to America more than two centuries ago was the herbaceous perennial, *Paeonia officinalis*, which has varieties with single and double crimson blossoms. After the middle 1700s, two other species from Asia were added: *Paeonia tenuifolia*, with delicate, fernlike leaves and deep crimson single and double blossoms, and the double white *Paeonia lactiflora (P. albiflora)*. By the early 1800s the peony had become one of the most admired garden plants. "Almost every village garden possesses a clump of the roots," a Bostonian wrote in 1837, "and the little parterres in front of cottages, by the road sides, throughout the country, are decked with its gay blossoms in the month of June." Often they were called by the old country name of "pinys," and the word is still occasionally heard. After generations, the plant became a symbol of old-fashioned gardens, rich with family memories, and was one of the plants most sadly missed by pioneer housewives who moved west. More recently its associative memories have been strengthened by its almost universal use on Memorial Day and as decorations in churches and for school commencements throughout rural America.

Beginning in the early 1800s other herbaceous peonies began coming from China. These included two of those shown on the opposite page: the double-red *Paeonia Pottsii* which was brought to Europe in 1822 and reported flowering in a Salem, Massachusetts, garden about 1838; and the flesh-colored *Paeonia Carnea*, introduced by a Parisian grower in 1852. The new plants encouraged French, Belgian, and some American plant breeders to develop new varieties, such as the *Compte de Paris*, also illustrated, developed by Modeste Guerin in Paris in 1842. In 1844 the Prince Nursery had ninety varieties for sale including *Paeonia Pottsii*. Before the end of the century there were more than 1,000 named varieties; in 1943 the list had grown to over 3,500.

After the Civil War, the herbaceous peony passed from fashion for a time, but its popularity among most American gardeners never wavered, and it has continued to brighten dooryard gardens throughout the country. Often it is the only surviving evidence of forgotten and overgrown rural gardens and house sites, enduring weeds and neglect, its showy blossoms and unforgettable musky scent providing a living tie with the past.

Chinese Paeonias

P. Carnea, Paeonia carnea triumphans   *P. Pottsii, Paeonia pottsi*

P. Compte de Paris, Paeonia comte deparis

Lithograph outline, watercolor, c. 1864, 28.2 ×
22.2 cm.

To Victorian ladies roses were not only objects of beauty, used to adorn their houses and persons, but flowers of great sentiment and symbolism, the inheritance of lore from centuries during which the rose was admired. Rose petals were used to make perfumes and a delicate flavoring and to freshen the air; they could be made into ointments or mixed with vinegar and honey to cure headaches, sore throats, and constipation. Made into beads or dried as potpourris, their fragrance could be preserved. They were also pressed between the leaves of diaries or autograph albums for remembrance, as many of these fragile souvenirs testify. In the unspoken "language of flowers," roses could be used to say a great deal, sparing one from writing a difficult letter or saying unpleasant things. A withered white rose was understood to mean "Emblem of my heart. Withered like your love." Yellow roses signified infidelity, causing one to wonder how and where they were used. There were also stories that the scent of roses could be dangerous. It was reported that roses in sleeping rooms "often occasioned serious injury," causing one writer to observe that "the most beautiful things in life contained the elements of death."

During the early nineteenth century, plant collectors sent roses to Western Europe from Asia and other parts of the world. These were soon hybridized with other species to form innumerable new forms and types, a process that has been energetically continued ever since. One of these introductions was an accidental seedling, found growing on the Isle de Bourbon (now Reunion Island) in the Indian Ocean, a cross between a China rose and one of the old Damask perpetuals. Plants of this hybrid sent to the gardens at Neuilly, France, became the parent of a new race admired for their habit of blooming throughout the season and for the size, perfection, and color of their blossoms. One of the numerous offspring was the "Souvenir de la Malmaison," developed by Jean Beluze, a nurseryman at Lyons, France, in 1843. Within a few years it was being grown in America and was described as "the most perfect and superb rose of this or any other class." Its very large and very double blossoms had thick, velvety petals of a light, transparent rose color. Presumably it was fragrant, although no writer bothered to mention it, but a rose then without fragrance would have been inconceivable. American growers were pleased with its hardiness, reporting that it could be grown in Albany and Boston, and in the Southern states. It is still a favorite among specialists, and plants can be obtained from nurseries dealing in old-fashioned roses.

Souvenir de la Malmaison Rose

Pencil, ink, theorem painting, watercolor, c. 1859,
28.7 × 22 cm.

"Strawberry. A Pledge of future happiness."—The
language of flowers, quoted by Mrs. Almira H. Lincoln
in *Familiar Lectures on Botany.*

Wild strawberries are found in many parts of the world, but they were not developed until long after many other fruits. Only a few improved varieties were grown in American gardens during the eighteenth and early nineteenth centuries before this neglected fruit became the subject of great interest among horticulturists. Much of this activity was stimulated by the new scientific knowledge that was beginning to transform the Victorian world, and which included the greater understanding of plant physiology and soil chemistry. During the 1840s the experimenting, breeding, and publication of experiments and theories reached such intensity that it was remembered as "The Great Strawberry Controversy." Out of it came some important results, particularly in furthering the breeding of improved varieties and better methods of cultivation, which, in turn, encouraged the commercial growth of strawberries near cities. Experimenters found, however, that while it was not difficult to create strains producing large berries and a heavy yield, the sweetness and aroma of the wild berries was often lost in the process. For anyone who has tasted the wild fruit, that is a very serious loss indeed. Nevertheless, berries of acceptable quality were developed, and the public, hungry for the fruit, agreed with Andrew Jackson Downing that strawberries were "Arcadian dainties with a true paradisical flavour." Some 54,000 bushels were sold in New York City in 1855.

The first really good strawberry in American gardens was Hovey's Seedling, developed between 1832 and 1838 by the distinguished Boston horticulturist and editor, Charles Mason Hovey. Hovey explained that he had been dissatisfied with the major varieties available at the time and decided to create a better one. Among the hundreds of plants he grew and tested was one that produced heavy crops of "dark rich shining red" berries with firm scarlet flesh, "abounding with a most agreeable acid, and exceedingly delicious and high-flavored juice." Berries of this variety grown for show purposes often measured from five to eight inches in circumference. Hovey's Seedling was soon grown in all parts of the country and sold for twice the price of any other variety. As late as 1880 it was still the standard variety, but as new ones appeared, it was gradually superseded. By 1925 there were some 1,362 named varieties of strawberries on record; more have been added since.

Hovey's Seedling Strawberry

Theorem painting, watercolor, glazed, c. 1859,
28.7 × 22 cm.

When D. W. Herstine of Philadelphia invited a group of distinguished horticulturists to visit his grounds on July 6, 1870, and examine his four new varieties of seedling raspberries, it was with the hope that those plants, or at least one of them, would meet standards of flavor, hardiness, and productivity lacking in the varieties then being grown. One of these, which came to be named "Herstine Red," did meet those requirements. The fruit was of very good quality, the canes had a strong growth, and it was very productive. But in the initial enthusiasm for this delicious berry, one important element was overlooked. The fruit was too soft to market successfully, and because of that the Herstine Red had only a moment of acclaim and disappeared within a few years.

Berries were the last of the fruits to receive the attention of American plant breeders or to be grown commercially, and of these the raspberry received the most belated attention. From very early in the colonial period European varieties were grown in some American gardens, but they did not take kindly to the American climate, lacking hardiness and productivity, although their fruit was superior. Furthermore, bushes of the sweet native American raspberry, and its cousin the blackberry, and others were abundant throughout much of the continent, growing in abandoned fields, on the edges of clearings, and along roadsides as they do today. Some colonists transplanted wild red raspberries into their gardens, and one of these, known as the "Common Red," was long in general cultivation.

Near the middle of the nineteenth century some American plant breeders began to develop new varieties, but with only limited success. The red and black raspberries grown today, both commercially and in home gardens, are largely the product of developments made during the past seventy-five years.

Herstine Red Raspberry

Theorem painting, watercolor, c. 1870s, 22 ×
14 cm.

"In France and England, the present rage for roses is intense," Francis Parkman, the American historian and horticulturist, wrote in 1866, adding that the new species brought from various parts of the globe, including America, were providing plant breeders with unusual opportunities to create new varieties of great beauty. Much of this experimental work was centered in France, where, as elsewhere, efforts were directed toward creating roses with a greater frequency of bloom throughout the season. The hybrid perpetuals, or "Remontant" roses as they were called in France, were the first major development, for they bloomed intermittently through the summer and autumn. They became immensely popular and in America were the dominant roses until the hybrid teas were developed later. Parkman referred to them as "a race of brilliant *parvenus*," adding that they "have risen to throw other roses into the shade. As we look upon them, we survey a gorgeous chaos . . . perplexing us in our search for genealogies and relationships.

One of the favorite perpetuals was the Baronne Prevost, which originated in France in 1842 and was being grown in America shortly afterward. It proved to be a hardy, vigorous grower with rich foliage, producing very fragrant, large double blossoms of a "light rose-color." It is still being grown.

Baronne Prevost Rose

Lithograph outline, watercolor, glazed, c. 1864,
26.7 × 17 cm.

"Dahlia. Forever thine."—The language of flowers,
quoted by Mrs. Almira H. Lincoln in *Familiar Lectures
on Botany.*

The flowers we usually think of as old-fashioned are those familiar friends which have been cultivated for generations, whose faces, forms, and habits have remained unchanged through the years, or relatively so. One can't claim that kind of familiarity with Dahlias, for they have been so constantly "improved" for more than a century and a half that they seem a procession of strangers marching through our gardens. Each year we may admire the dazzling qualities of the newcomers, or be intimidated by their size and self-assurance, but before they become friends another year brings strangers of their tribe to take their place. Few plants have been so completely or so ceaselessly transformed as these.

The native species was brought from Mexico to Madrid in 1789. Linnaeus named it for one of his pupils, Andreas Dahl. It must have been an unprepossessing plant with rather uninteresting single blossoms and a slovenly plant form, but plant breeders became interested in its possibilities because the flowers came in a wide range of colors and tended to double under cultivation. Beginning their work about 1814, they produced gorgeous new blossoms within a very short time, disciplined the plant's form, and greatly extended the period of bloom. In America by the 1830s "the surpassing beauty and brilliancy" of these new flowers had captivated the "curious and the wealthy," along with "the humble admirer of nature's abortive wonders." The rich colors and the formality of the flowers, which a later writer rather unkindly described as being round and hard and stiff as a ball, appealed to the taste of the times. They were also relatively inexpensive. In 1838 George C. Thorburn, a New York seedsman, offered a choice selection of twenty-five double varieties for twenty dollars. The colors then being grown were: variegated, white, yellow, scarlet, crimson, maroon, rose, purple, and lilac. An example of the last is here illustrated. By 1841 one English dealer had over 1,000 varieties in cultivation. In the years since then the named varieties have proliferated.

For exhibition purposes, the flowers were first classified as "Show" and "Fancy," the former being those of a single color and the latter variegated. When the cycle of taste changed from formality to informality after the Civil War, the Dahlia declined in popularity until new and freer forms were introduced about 1879, and interest in the single form revived a few years later. Since then the Dahlia has remained one of the most widely cultivated American garden flowers.

Dahlia

Penciled outline, watercolor, c. 1859, 28.7 ×
22 cm.

"Althea. I would not act contrary to reason."—The
language of flowers, quoted by Mrs. Almira H. Lincoln
in *Familiar Lectures on Botany.*

The Althea has been grown in America for perhaps two centuries. It is a hardy
shrub, undemanding, resistant to most of the ills that affect other plants, and
blossoms profusely during August and September when few other shrubs
flower. Its unscented blossoms are in shades of white, red, blue, and purple.
There are single and double varieties and others with variegated petals. So many
virtues would lead one to assume that the Althea is one of the most familiar and
beloved American shrubs. Familiar it is, but scarcely beloved. It was generally
ignored by early horticulturists and garden writers. Specimens are common in old
gardens, but often these are a singularly unattractive variety with bluish-lavender
petals and a red center, although more attractive colors have been available at
nurseries for generations. The Landreth Nursery in Philadelphia offered six
varieties in 1811. Parsons & Co., at Flushing, Long Island, had four varieties in
1843, including a double red and a white one streaked with red which was called
"Painted Lady." Ten years later they were still offering the same varieties, suggesting that sales were limited. However the Prince Nursery, also at Flushing,
offered thirty-one varieties in 1860, including many shades of red with double
blossoms. The names and descriptions given in the catalogs were confusing and
conflicting, as a writer complained with reason. Was the correct name "Pleasant
Eye" or "Pheasant Eye"? Both appeared in early catalogs with determined
persistence.

The Althea, from the Greek word meaning *cure* and implying its early use in
medicine, is a native of China and India and was brought to Europe before 1600.
How it camed to be called "Rose of Sharon" in America seems to be unrecorded,
but it has been known by that name for generations. In England the "Rose of
Sharon" is a very different shrub, *Hypericum calycinum.*

Double Althea
Hibiscus syriacus

Theorem painting, watercolor, c. 1870s, 22 ×
14 cm.

The peach is not native to North America and was first introduced by the Spaniards in Florida and Mexico. The Indians became so fond of the fruit that, by the time the first English settlements were made along the East Coast, peach trees were found growing in Indian villages as far north as they would grow, and west to the present states of Arkansas and Texas. The fruit seems to have been of very poor quality, but the trees bore abundantly, as William Penn commented in 1683.

After improved varieties from Western Europe were imported, natural and artificially-produced hybrids began to appear in American orchards. Much later these were greatly increased by the introduction in 1850 of the Chinese Cling group by Charles Downing (1802-1885), brother of Andrew Jackson Downing, and the Chinese Peento or Java peach, by the Berckmans nursery, Fruitland, at Augusta, Georgia, in 1869.

Sometime after 1800, William Crawford of Middletown, New Jersey, produced two fine new peaches, Crawford's Early and Crawford's Late. The former, a large freestone peach with yellow flesh ripening in August, was described by William Kenrick in 1841. "Its melting flesh and luscious flavor" soon made it the most prized of the early yellow peaches, and for almost fifty years it was one of the principal varieties grown and sold commercially.

Beginning in the 1840s peach culture boomed, but the contagious plant disease, "the yellows," soon decimated orchards in state after state. After the disease had run its course, new orchards were planted, many with varieties more resistant to the yellows than the earlier ones, but it must be lamented that those which now best meet marketing requirements are seldom either "luscious" or "melting."

Crawford's Early Peach

Theorem painting, watercolor, c. 1864, 28.2 ×
22.2 cm.

"Wild Grape. Charity."—The language of flowers, quoted in *Flora's Dictionary*, by a Lady [Mrs. Elizabeth Wirt].

Beginning with the first European settlement of North America, repeated efforts were made to introduce European grapes. The vines flourished for a few years but then mysteriously died. It was not until the early 1870s that the cause was traced to Phylloxera, a native aphid very destructive to grape vines, to which the American grapes were resistant. Only along the Pactific Coast, where this insect was absent, could the European varieties be grown, and this was one of the principal reasons for the growth of the California grape industry. Elsewhere growers found success only with improved varieties of native grapes and hybrids of American and European varieties. Among those developed before 1850 were the Catawba, Delaware, Norton's Virginia Seedling, and Isabella. Names always imply something about the mood of a period. Near the middle of the century many of the new grapes were given feminine names: Anna, Hagar, Diana, Lydia, Cloantha, and others—including Martha, a Concord seedling. The last was developed sometime before 1864 by Samuel Miller (1820-1901), who named it for his wife. Miller was then living in Lebanon County, Pennsylvania, where his work as an experimental horticulturist was beginning to attract attention among his colleagues throughout the country. His new grape created considerable interest because of its beautiful pale greenish-yellow fruit and large, juicy, and sweet berries, as well as for its vigorous growth. It proved excellent for the table and for its light, straw-colored, delicately flavored wine. Miller was one of those useful men so intensely interested in his experimental work that he spent his life in developing new varieties of fruits and berries and in freely sharing his knowledge with others in the field. "I have no time to make money," he declared late in life, but others benefitted, as did the Pittsburgh nurserymen J. Knox, to whom Miller transferred his stock of the Martha grape for propagation and sale.

In 1867 Miller moved to Bluffton, Montgomery County, Missouri, as superintendent of the newly formed Bluffton Wine Company. After its failure several years later, he continued his experiments and was an active participant in horticultural affairs during the remainder of the century.

The Martha grape remained popular for several decades, but in time was replaced by new varieties, particularly the Niagara.

Martha Grape

Theorem painting, watercolor, c. 1870s, 22 ×
14 cm.

Near the end of his life, Ephraim W. Bull, an unassuming resident of Concord, Massachusetts, told of developing America's best-known grape. In his yard he had found a seedling vine, apparently brought in from the woods by a previous owner, which had such large, sweet fruit that he decided to experiment with its improvement. After many years of painstaking selection from hundreds of seedlings, he produced the Concord in 1849 and first exhibited it at the Massachusetts Horticultural Society in 1853. Its "extreme hardiness, vigor, and productiveness of the vine, and the large size and fine appearance of the bunches and berries" met many of the requirements long sought by home growers and the wine industry. People liked the flavor of the fresh fruit, housewives found it excellent for jellies and conserves, and it made a pleasant light-red wine which, one writer said, "is effectually becoming the laboring man's drink; can be produced cheap enough, is very palatable, and has a peculiar, refreshing effect on the system."

Despite its popular success, the experts pointed out that the grape's flavor was not first-rate and that the fruit was too tender to ship long distances. This was true enough but, as Orange Judd, the editor of *The American Agriculturist*, reminded the critics, "It was a grape, and one who had a Concord vine was sure to have grapes—not the best that could be imagined, but eatable and acceptable, and vastly better than no grapes." He had observed from his travels that the farther west it was grown the better it was, and mentioned the sweetness and abundance of the fruit he had seen in the Hermann, Missouri, vineyards which, before prohibition, supplied the town's large wine industry.

Ephraim Bull, who had revolutionized grape culture in America, received few honors and little reward for his work. A photograph of his standing beside his original Concord vine shows a rather shy-looking man, below average in height, wearing a full white beard and work clothes which included a long apron and a bowler hat. He died in poverty at Concord in 1895.

Concord Grape

Lithograph, applied color, glazed, c. 1859, 28.7 ×
22 cm.

Plums vary so greatly in their forms, colors, texture, and flavors, and are so easily hybridized, that the fruit has been a favorite among growers for centuries. More than 2,000 varieties have been grown in America, all developed from some fifteen native and European species. Indians were very fond of the native plum, of which the beach plum, the sloe or Allegheny plum, and the Chickasaw plum are the main species. From selecting and growing the best specimens found in the wild, the Indians developed varieties which the European settlers also came to prize, particularly the Chickasaw plum, which was grown in many orchards during the eighteenth century. Soon after 1800 two named varieties of wild plums of Midwestern origin became popular, the Miner and the Wild Goose, grown from a seed dropped by a goose. Among the European varieties introduced was the Green Gage, the Reine Claude of France, where it appears to have originated in the sixteenth century. Here it became, and remains, a favorite because of its "melting, juicy and exquisitely flavoured" green flesh, as described by William Coxe in 1817.

About 1825, Judge Jesse Buel of Rochester, New York, developed and named the Jefferson, which, when it was introduced to general cultivation in the 1840s, became a rival of the Green Gage. All writers spoke of the beauty of the fruit and its luscious, juicy flavor. It ripened the last of August and hung unusually long on the trees, a quality much prized by the early orchardists. Furthermore, it was less liable to the attacks of wasps, which often destroyed other light-colored plums upon maturity.

After many years of popularity, the Jefferson plum was replaced by newer varieties, but the Green Gage plum still continues to be found in some orchards, its flavor, either fresh or stewed, delighting those who eat it.

Jefferson Plum

Theorem painting, watercolor, c. 1859, 28.7 ×
22 cm.

Currants and gooseberries belong to the same botanical family, and wild species of both are found in the Old and New Worlds. In North America the Indians traditionally used the native currants, particularly the black variety, *Ribes americanum*, in their diet, and early settlers followed their example. European varieties, developed in Northern Europe and Britain at an early period, were introduced by the early colonists. By the nineteenth century the berry was common in American gardens, except in the South, for it prefers a cool, moist climate. The imported varieties proved to be so hardy that they generally received little care and consequently returned poor crops, but these were perhaps sufficient for home needs. Like other berries, the currant was late in capturing the interest of commercial growers and plant breeders, perhaps because the fruit had such limited market value. Not until the 1830s did its cultivation and the development of new varieties begin to receive attention. The red varieties have always been the most popular for jelly, tarts, and pies, currant shrub, and a sweet wine which one writer reported was "very popular among farmers." Farm boys delighted in the ripe berries, and when picking them sometimes "soured the crop" by stuffing themselves with the fruit. For those suffering from "febrile disease" (feverish disorders), a cool drink made from the jelly was recommended.

But what of the white currants? They figure in none of the recipes or reminiscences of the writers, and yet from the 1830s until after 1900, the White Grape Currant, a European variety sometimes called Transparent White, was among those most highly recommended, particularly for home gardens. It was included among the fifty-five varieties offered for sale in 1860 by the Prince Nursery, priced at twenty-five cents each or two dollars for a dozen plants. The berries were described as being "very large, whitish yellow, sweet and good: very productive; moderately long bunches."

After the Civil War, growing currants declined because of the spread of various insect pests and plant diseases, particularly the imported currant worm, which stripped the leaves from neglected bushes throughout the eastern United States. It was also found that currents are alternating hosts for the white-pine blisterrust, and, as noted earlier, their growth has been outlawed in many states.

Some varieties of currants grown as ornamentals (*see* p. 33) also produce fruit which has a limited use, but most of these are not very productive, nor do their berries have the quality of the fruiting varieties.

White Grape Currant

Theorem painting, watercolor, c. 1864, 28.2 × 22.2 cm.

The Seckel (or Seckle, as it was sometimes spelled) originated on the outskirts of Philadelphia about the 1760s under circumstances related by a number of eminent colonial authorities. Although their accounts vary considerably in detail, it appears that the original tree may have been a seedling from the Swedish settlement established before Penn's arrival. It was found growing in the Southern part of what later became Philadelphia, near Girard Point, on a farm owned by Jacob Weiss, otherwise known as Dutch Weiss, a "well-known sporting character." Later the farm was purchased by a Mr. Seckel (or Seckle), who recognized the value of the fruit and brought it to public attention. It became so popular that for almost a century Seckel pears, along with the White Doyenne or Butter pear, were the most popular varieties sold in the Philadelphia markets. William Coxe, the first to write of it in his *View of the Cultivation of Fruit Trees* (1817) and a man ordinarily restrained in his enthusiasms, asserted that it "is in the general estimation of amateurs of fine fruit, both natives and foreigners, the finest pear of this or any other country. . . . The size generally is small, the form regular . . . the skin is sometimes yellow, with a bright red cheek, and smooth; at other times a perfect russet, without any blush—the flesh is melting, juicy, and most exquisitely and delicately flavoured; the time of ripening is from the end of August, to the middle of October." Its "high musky perfume" caused some comment among later writers, one finding that "its flavour is very peculiar, having a factitious aromatick perfume rather than the odour or taste of fruits." The public, however, was unconcerned by such nuances. Generations of Americans have delighted in this sweet and juicy fruit, and it is still being grown in some home and commercial orchards.

Seckel Pear

Theorem painting, watercolor, c. 1870s, 22 $\times$ 14 cm.

The English climate, unlike that of America, is admirably suited to growing large and delicious gooseberries, and there the fruit has been popular for a long time, both for cooking when green and as a dessert fruit when ripe. Unfortunately the English varieties proved very susceptible to mildew in this country, so that the plants became worthless soon after coming into bearing. Our native species, immune to mildew, grow abundantly in many parts of the country and for a long time were used by country families, even though they found picking the small berries from the tangled bushes, with their prickly spines, a tedious, painful chore. Consequently, gooseberries were little grown in American gardens until the early 1830s, when Abel Houghton, at Lynn, Massachusetts, crossed a native variety (said to have been *Ribes hirtellum*, the Smooth or Hairystem Gooseberry), with an imported variety. The result was a mildew-resistant plant producing small berries of fine flavor in extraordinary profusion. This new variety stimulated the home and, to a limited extent, the commercial growing of the fruit, a trend later encouraged by a seedling of the Houghton that Charles Downing developed about 1855 at his Newburgh, New York, nursery. Downing's Seedling had many fine qualities including large berries with thin skins and "a delicate sweet vinous flavor, like the finest foreign varieties." It was soon introduced by various nurseries, resulting in a flurry of interest among cultivators. It remained a favorite until after 1900 and may still be grown. Other improved varieties soon followed.

Some growers sought to emulate English gardeners by producing immense berries by special cultivation. In 1860 and 1861 gooseberry shows were held at Paterson, New Jersey, at which a number of growers competed. Some entries weighed considerably more than an ounce each. Similar specimens sent to the editor of *The American Agriculturist* averaged four and one-half inches in circumference and looked like "mammoth plums." Despite the spate of attention, gooseberries did not develop a widespread popularity among commercial growers and continued to be grown primarily as a home crop. Each decade new pests were reported. For many families, particularly those recently from Europe, gooseberries continued to be popular. Picked green, the berries were used for canning and making jam, spiced gooseberries, or the rich dessert "Gooseberry Fool," but their small size has precluded their use here as a dessert fruit.

Downing's Seedling Gooseberry

Theorem painting, watercolor, c. 1870s, 22 ×
14 cm.

"This apple is called in New York the Lady apple from the beauty of its appearance," wrote William Coxe of Burlington, New Jersey, in his *View of the Cultivation of Fruit Trees*, the first American work on that subject. It is one of the oldest varieties of apples still in cultivation, having originated in France, where it is known by various names, principally Pomme d'Apis. When it was first grown in America is unrecorded, but it was found in orchards during the last half of the eighteenth century. The Prince Nursery offered it for sale in 1790 and continued to stock it until after 1860. Their catalog for the latter year described it as "quite small, flat, uniform, brilliant deep red cheek on light yellow flesh, tender, crisp, juicy, mild, slight subacid, good flavor, a beautiful fancy apple for parties, commands twice the price of any other apple; growth vigorous but not rapid, forms a beautiful regular conical tree with luxuriant foliage." It ripens late in the autumn and, with care, can be preserved for use until late in the following spring.

The Lady apple has always been considered a "fancy fruit." In 1854 it was reported that the apple commanded a high price, both in American cities and in London, "for fashionable evening parties," one Dutchess County, New York, farmer selling his crop at from nine to ten dollars a bushel. The fruit is still being grown commercially and still selling at high prices, usually through gourmet food stores in the larger cities for table decorations and gift baskets. Unfortunately Lady apple cider may be only a nostalgic memory. Properly made with loving care and fermented under controlled conditions, it had an unforgettable champagne quality that added something very special to festive occasions.

Lady Apple

Theorem painting, watercolor, c. 1870s, 22 ×
14 cm.

"Anemone. Anticipation. Frailty."—The language of flowers, quoted by Mrs. Almira H. Lincoln in *Familiar Lectures on Botany.*

The Japanese anemone was among the plants brought by Robert Fortune, the Scottish botanist, from China to England in 1846. The following year a specimen bloomed in the Boston garden of Charles Mason Hovey, horticulturist and editor of America's first successful gardening journal, *The Magazine of Horticulture.* Hovey was delighted with it. "It possesses a neat and ample foliage," he wrote, "and its pale rosy semi-double flowers" were on "terminal clusters on tall stems that rise above the leaves." He pronounced it a valuable addition to the small number of plants flowering late in the autumn and added that this herbaceous, hardy plant was easily cultivated. Such high praise from a respected authority should have made it welcomed by gardeners, but most American writers of the period either ignored the plant or mentioned it only briefly. Perhaps it was too modest in appearance to compete for public interest with the showier Chrysanthemums that had come to dominate the autumn gardens. Whatever the reason, the Japanese anemone, with its charming pink and white blossoms, has never been widely grown by American gardeners.

Anemone Japonica

Anemone hupehensis japonica

Theorem painting, watercolor, c. 1870s, 22 ×
14 cm.

A Note on the Illustration Sources

The plates for *A Nineteenth-Century Garden* are drawn from four different primary sources, including: D. M. Dewey, *The Colored Fruit Book for the Use of Nurserymen*, Rochester, N.Y., 1859—Northern Spy Apple, New American Weeping Willow, Forsythia and Ribes Beatone, Bleeding Heart, Double White-Flowering Almond and Double Crimson-Flowering Peach, Hovey's Seedling Strawberry, Souvenir de la Malmaison Rose, Dahlia, Concord Grape, and Jefferson Plum; an untitled bound collection of plates, c. 1870—Tulips, Chinese Paeonias, White Fringe Tree, Baronne Prevost Rose, Crawford's Early Peach, and White Grape Currant; a book of plates assembled after 1888 for an agent of the Continental Nurseries, Rochester, N.Y.—Weigela Florabunda, Double Althea, and Anemone Japonica; and a book of plates assembled after 1875 for J. W. Adams, Brightwood Nursery, Springfield, Mass.—Herstine Red Raspberry, Martha Grape, Downing's Seedling Gooseberry, Seckel Pear, and Lady Apple.

A Bibliographic Note

This study, including the illustrations, is based on material in my personal collection. Those readers wishing to explore the subject further would find, as I have, the following references helpful. Unfortunately, copies of the earlier titles, particularly catalogs, which are essential to any study of American horticulture, are only to be found in a few specialized libraries.

The large number of American agricultural and horticultural magazines published during the nineteenth century make fascinating reading today. Many were short-lived, but the best of them provide data on plant introductions and changing gardening tastes found nowhere else. Especially informative are the *Magazine of Horticulture* (Boston, 1835-1869); *Horticulturist and Journal of Rural Art and Rural Taste* (Albany, etc., 1846-1875); Thomas Meehan's *Gardener's Monthly and Horticultural Advertiser* (Philadelphia, 1859-1875), and its successors, *The Gardener's Monthly and Horticulturist* (1876-1888), and *Meehan's Monthly* (1891-1902); *Garden and Forest* (New York, 1888-1897); *Vick's Illustrated Magazine*, etc. (Rochester, 1878-1900); and the *American Agriculturist* (New York, etc., particularly for the years 1842-1885).

Contemporary descriptions of plants, their cultivation, garden design, and much else are in Joseph Breck, *The Flower Garden* (1856); William Coxe, *A View of the Cultivation of Fruit Trees* (1817); Andrew Jackson Downing, *The Fruit and Fruit Trees of America* (1845, 1860 eds.), and *A Treatise on the Theory and Practice of Landscape Gardening, Adapted to North America* (1853, 1859 eds.); Andrew S. Fuller, *The Grape Culturist* (1864), and *The Small Fruit Culturist* (1867, 1894 eds.); U. P. Hedrick, *Cyclopedia of Hardy Fruits* (1922); Peter Henderson, *Henderson's Handbook of Plants* (1881); Charles Mason Hovey, *The Fruits of America* (1851-1856); William Kenrick, *The New American Orchardist* (1848); J. C. Loudon, *Arboretum et Fruticetum Britannicum* (1854); Bernard M'Mahon, *The American Gardener's Calendar* (1806); Francis Parkman, *The Book of Roses* (1866); S. B. Parsons, *The Rose* (1847); Edward Sayers, *The American Flower Garden Companion* (1838); James Thacher, *American Orchardist* (1822); and John J. Thomas, *American Fruit Culturist* (1849, 1875 eds.). For vegetables, *Field and Garden Vegetables*, by Fearing Burr, Jr. (1863), is the most informative.

Subtleties in the language of flowers are explained by Mrs. Almira H. Lincoln, *Familiar Lectures on Botany* (1831); Catherine H. Waterman, *Flora's Lexicon* (1840); and Mrs. Elizabeth Wirt, *Flora's Dictionary* (1833).

Standard works useful in unraveling the mysteries of botanical nomenclature are L. H. Bailey, ed., *Cyclopedia of American Horticulture* (1900); Harland P. Kelsey and William A. Dayton, eds., *Standardized Plant Names* (1942); E. L. Little, Jr., *Check-List of Native and Naturalized Trees of the United States* (U. S. Forest Service, 1953); and Alfred Rehder, *Manual of Cultivated Trees and Shrubs Hardy in North America* (1974).

Much about American horticultural history is found in Bailey's *Cyclopedia of American Horticulture* and is detailed in U. P. Hedrick's *History of Horticulture in America to 1860* (1950) and Ann Leighton's delightful *American Gardens in the Eighteenth Century* (1976).

Index

ISBN 0-87663-976-7

A Main Street Press Book   UNIVERSE BOOKS   New York